Contents

FlappyBird

Get Ready!

© Dong Nguyen 2013

Published 2014. Pedigree Books Limited, Beech Hill House, Walnut Gardens, Exeter, Devon EX4 4DH. www.pedigreebooks.com, books@pedigreegroup.co.uk
The Pedigree trademark, email and website addresses, are the sole and exclusive properties of Pedigree Group Limited, used under licence in this publication.

COLOUR IT

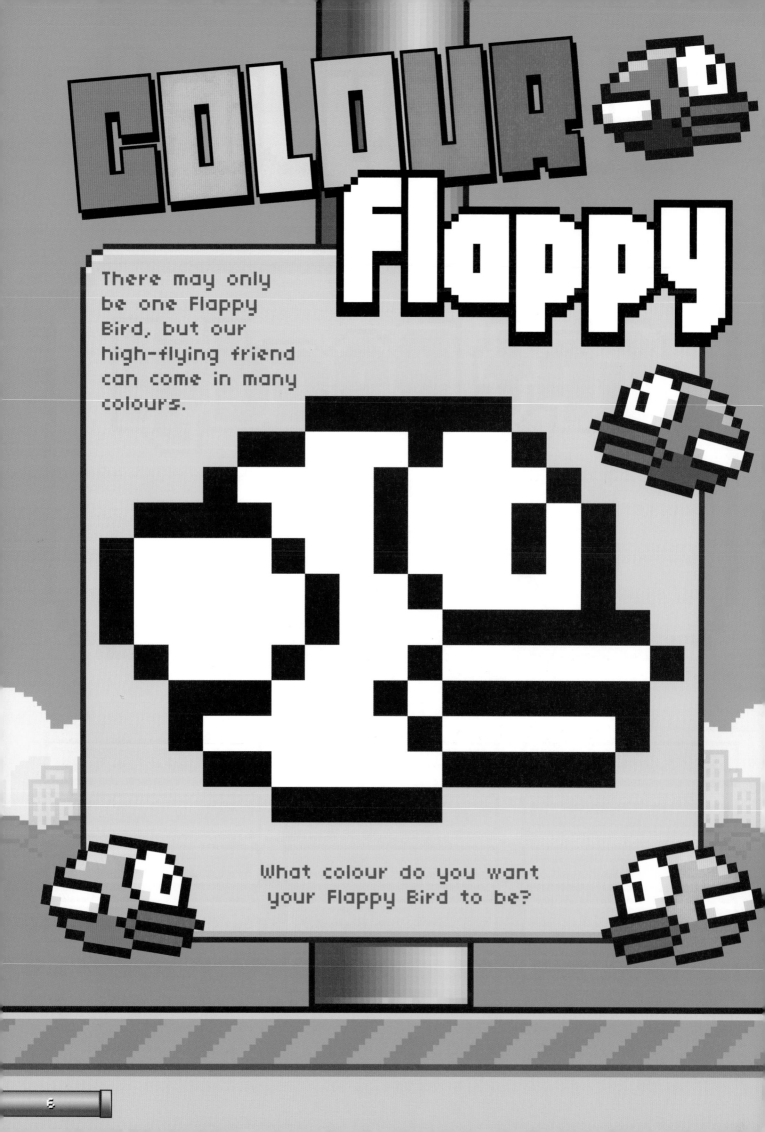

Flappy

There may only be one Flappy Bird, but our high-flying friend can come in many colours.

What colour do you want your Flappy Bird to be?

Bird SPOTTING

Can you spot your plucky playmates all in the right row? Find the correct sequence in this crazy pattern before the birdies crash!

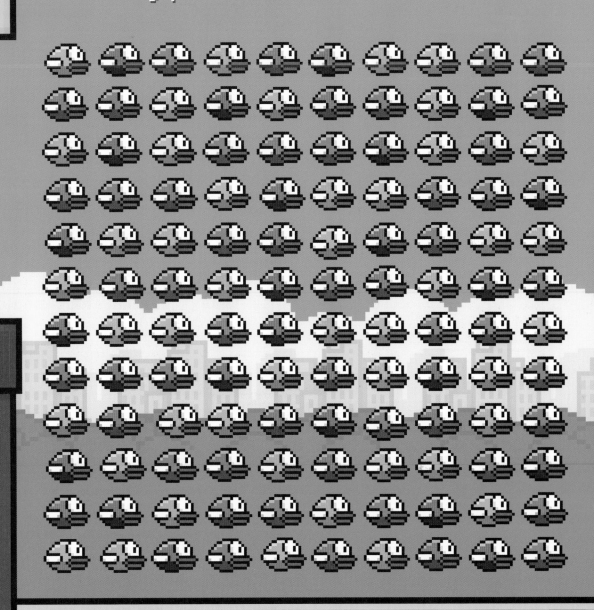

Tricky Turns

use your mettle to reach the medal!

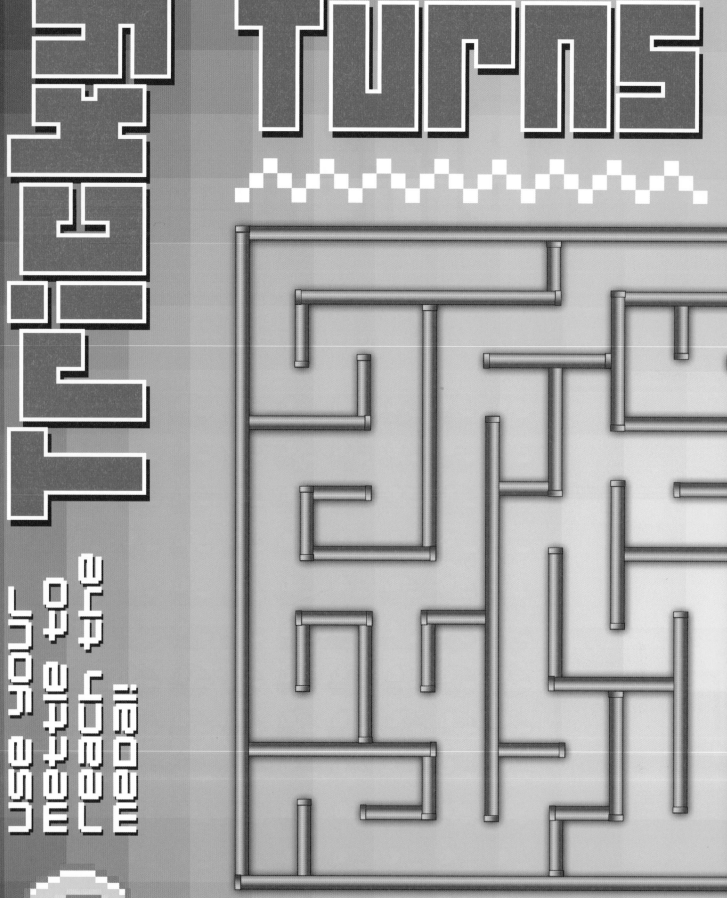

chirp as you jerk around the tricky tunnel!

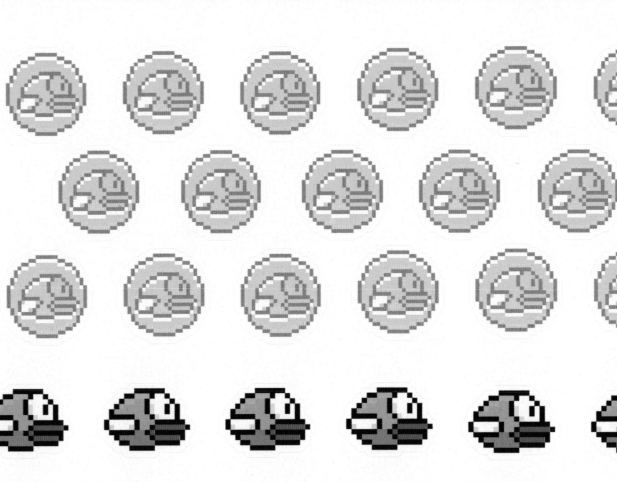

FlappyBird

FlappyBird

WHOOSH!!

KA-POW!

VROOOOM!

WHACK!

KA-POW!

WHOOSH!!

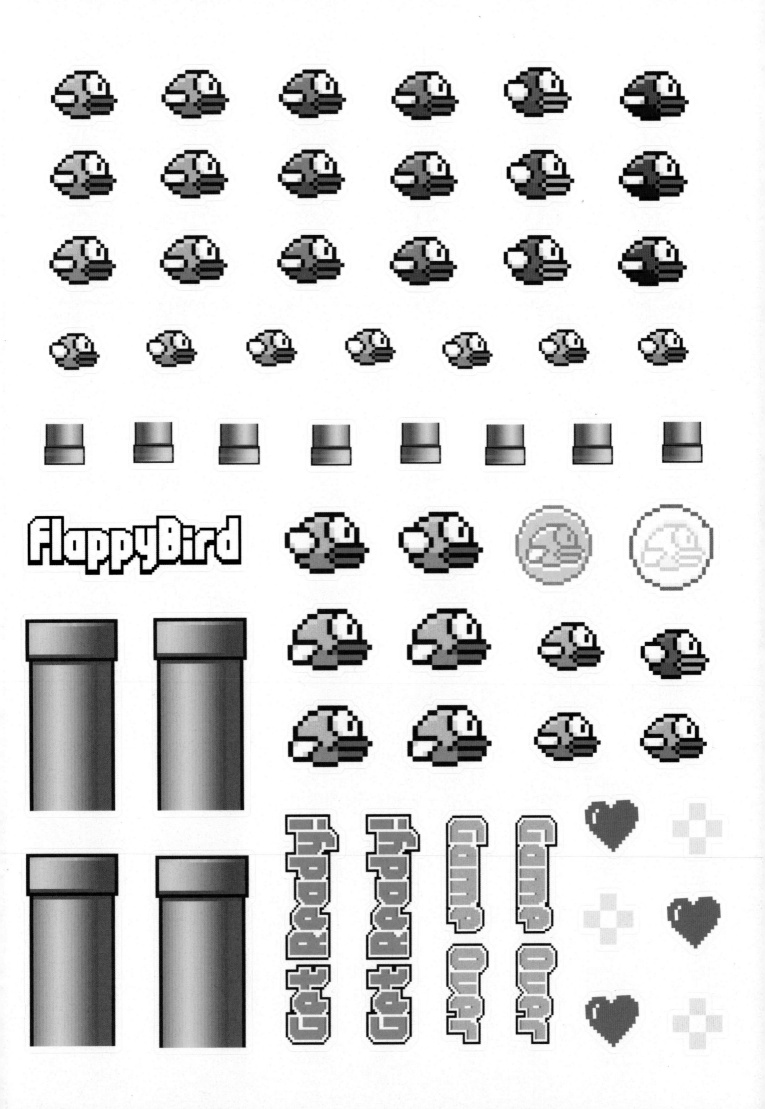

START

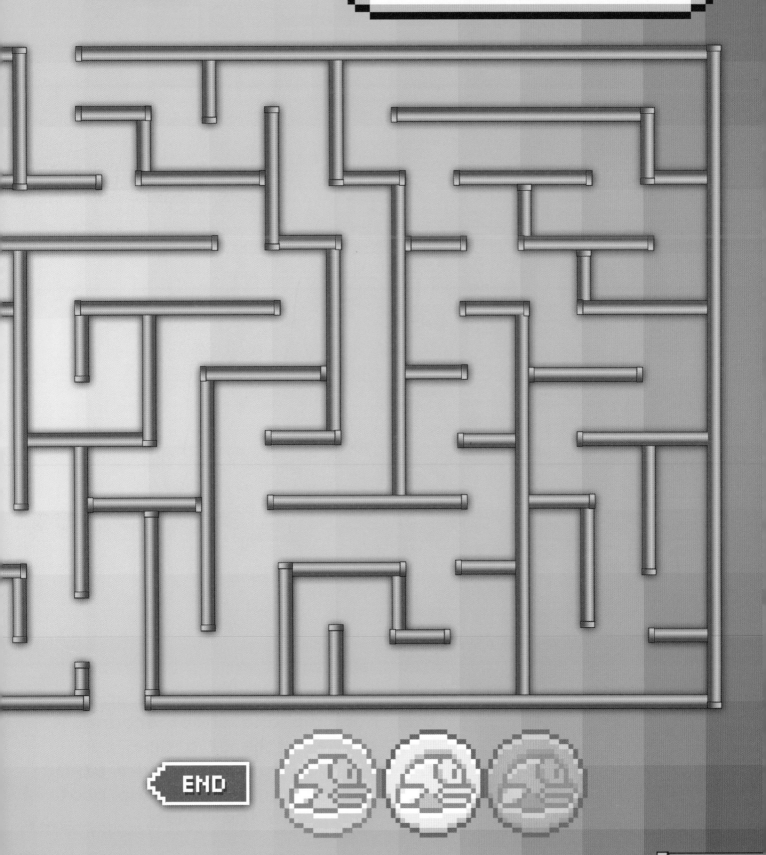

Help Flappy Bird stay on track through this mighty pipe puzzle to reach the medals. Use your finger to tap along the path and twist around the jutting network of traps to the prize.

END

Chirpy Crossing

A N G J P Y B K C P
M F P B M F P L Q F
L S P T C P F F U
B D U F P Y B R N B
F L A P E F M I R I
W F C P F X T G D D

10

KA-ching! Collect the medals as you fly.

Flappy Bird likes to hover and then hop, dip and shoot around. Moving one letter at a time, can you find a way to spell FLAPPY BIRD without breaking a chain? Help pilot Flappy to the finish!

Feather Find

A	S	F	U	N	N	Y	U	F	W	P	C	L	Q	T	O	H	F	A
D	K	B	S	C	W	P	N	A	R	S	B	I	F	G	X	L	O	K
F	E	A	C	Y	Z	A	F	L	I	P	C	J	F	D	Y	A	C	Y
H	D	Z	G	I	K	Q	A	P	S	K	F	L	W	E	F	P	X
F	Y	Q	F	E	B	O	R	Q	W	F	D	S	A	H	J	G	R	I	S
S	A	X	Y	L	C	B	K	T	S	H	K	S	O	P	Z	T	Y	R
Y	S	G	D	S	A	C	S	J	H	S	D	T	A	F	A	A	A	F
B	A	S	L	H	D	P	K	S	G	U	F	A	B	A	F	F	D	R
J	P	K	H	Y	L	S	P	U	H	P	C	A	I	G	M	L	H	L
T	B	P	A	U	R	J	Z	Y	R	A	D	I	F	K	N	O	A	C
E	D	E	F	M	E	H	H	M	S	M	L	E	H	C	I	A	E	O
E	I	W	R	G	N	W	S	J	W	F	M	A	I	L	A	T	P	N
L	F	A	T	X	Q	F	E	A	T	H	E	R	A	A	K	A	O	F
F	O	L	I	K	A	I	J	L	J	V	R	A	O	S	N	F	E	I
L	Q	F	H	R	F	J	Y	K	Y	B	H	F	P	M	K	D	R	D
G	P	A	G	F	G	C	S	H	I	R	G	O	B	Q	F	E	P	D
H	N	P	T	H	R	E	T	T	U	L	F	C	M	A	G	O	H	L
P	A	O	R	K	P	S	W	A	P	L	M	D	F	I	B	N	F	Y

Wrap your wings around this feathery wordsearch. How many words about Flappy Bird that begin with the letter F can you find? Look forwards, backwards, up, down and diagonally.

Feather   **Fleet**
Flappy   **Flip**
Fly   **Funny**
Float   **Fast**
Flutter   **Fiddly**

SILLY SPOTTING

FLAPPY FLIES FAST LIKE A SILLY WIND SURFER IN THE SKY, WEAVING UP AND DOWN THROUGH THE AIR. IT CAN GET A BIT DICEY WHEN DODGING PIPES. PRESS PAUSE! CAN YOU SPOT TEN DIFFERENCES BETWEEN THESE TWO FROZEN PICTURES?

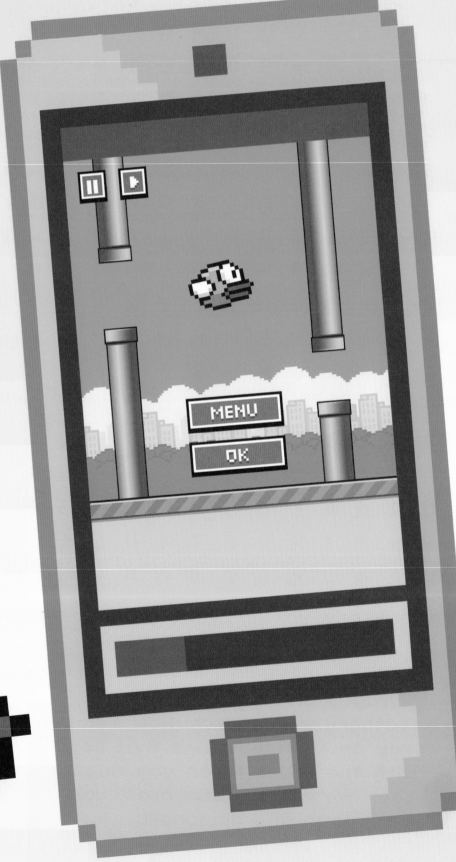

Get ready for a crash landing!

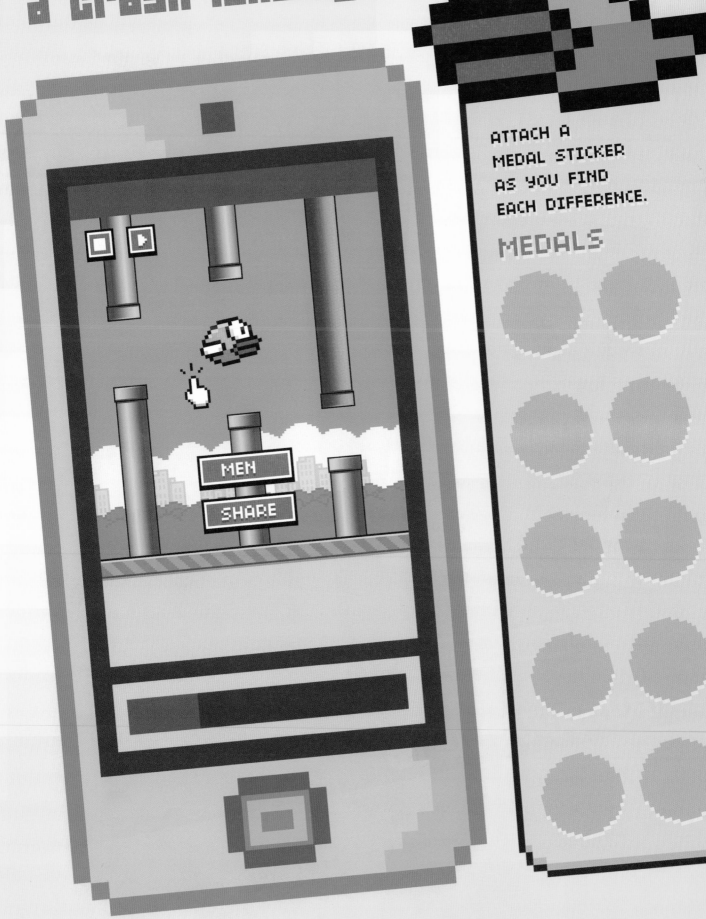

MEN

SHARE

ATTACH A MEDAL STICKER AS YOU FIND EACH DIFFERENCE.

MEDALS

pixelated plumes

Flappy is snap-happy at a plume party, but the images are pixelated. Use the clues to guess what kind of bird is in each picture, then remember the random bird facts to amaze your friends.

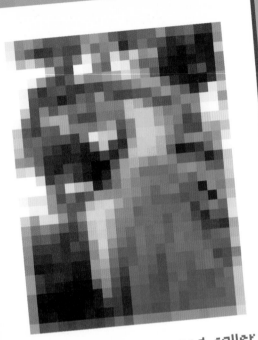

1. The brightly coloured caller that lives in the rainforest.

FLAMINGO

2. A wise-looking fluffy friend that likes to hunt at night.

FLAPPY FACTS

- Penguins are birds that can't fly.
- There are around 10,000 different species of birds worldwide.
- The ostrich is the largest and fastest bird on the planet.
- Hummingbirds can fly backwards.
- Some birds are clever enough to make and use tools.

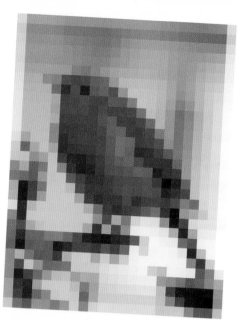

3. The chirpy chap with a red chest in your garden.

4. A soaring predator that commands a huge wingspan.

CROW

OWL

EAGLE

ROBIN

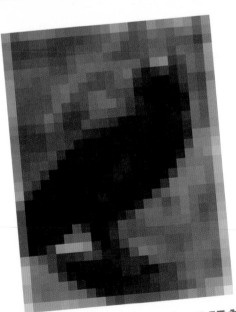

5. A black bird that's named after the call it makes that rhymes with 'mow'.

PARROT

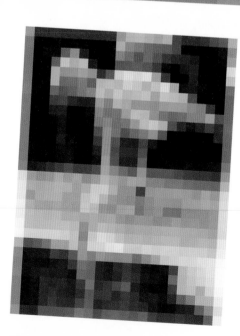

6. The bird that wades through rivers on stilt-like legs.

counting chaos

Wow, a treasure trove of medals! And here's a swarm of medal-hunting chirping chaps. Are there more medals than birds or more birds than medals?

Bird Words

Flappy can be dappy, but not wacky. How many words can you make from the letters in the phrase 'FLAPPY BIRD'?

Tap that billed brain and write the words you make below.

1. Flab Drippy

Target practice

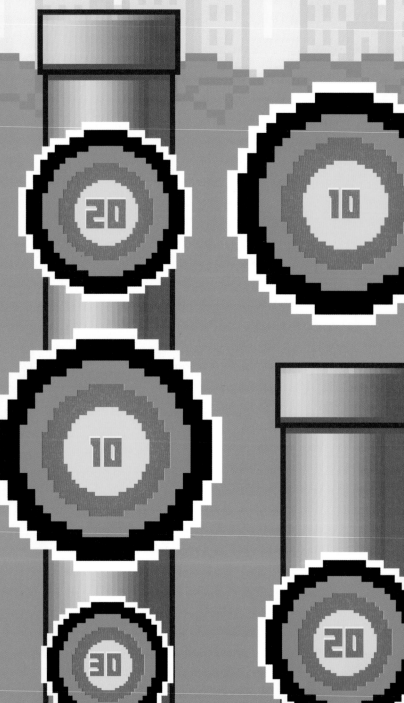

Does playing the Flappy Bird game get you in a funny flutter? On a scale of 1-10, with 1 being easy and 10 being dip-iculously hard, how would you rank the difficulty of the avian antics?

Here's a mock trial of the tough game world for target training. Close your eyes and use your stickers to practise hitting target zones. The smaller the target, the more points you score, but your tally will drop to zero if you stick Flappy on a pipe. Count up your score after five goes.

PIXEL Bird Food

String

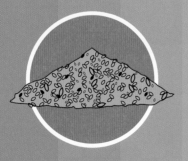

Bird seed

Peanut Butter

Ice-cube Tray

After all the constant zipping and zooming, birds are bound to get very hungry! Why don't you make some tasty treats for the flappy birds in your area More food = more flapping!

HOW TO MAKE:

STEP 1

Mix birdseed and peanut butter (or honey) until it's the texture of play-doh.

Spoon enough of the bird seed mixture into the mould to cover the bottom. Place the end of a piece of string in the centre of each mould then cover completely with the bird seed mixture.

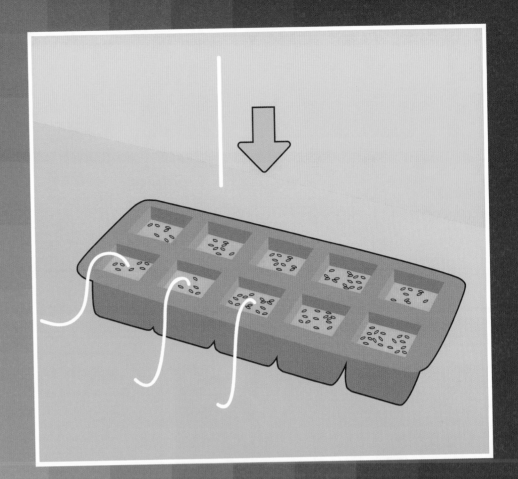

Freeze overnight.

Pop bird feeders out of moulds and hang outside (preferably on a cooler day, if it's too hot out, the peanut butter may melt!)

Odd Bird Out

Birds come in all shapes, sizes and colours
and live in different kinds of places.
Can you help Flappy Bird find out which
friend is the odd one out in each group?
Write your answers on the next page!

GROUP 1

GROUP 1

FLAPPY FACT

Woodpeckers can peck 20 times per second.

DUCK

WOODPECKER

GOOSE

SWAN

GROUP 2

PENGUIN

PELICAN

PUFFIN

PARROT

FLAPPY FACT

Parrots can live up to 80 years in the wild.

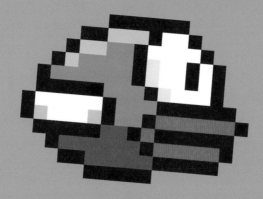

GROUP 3

GROUP 4

FLAPPY FACT

Harris hawks are unique because they hunt in a family pack.

HERON

KIWI

HARRIS HAWK

CURLEW

SPARROW

BLACKBIRD

STARLING

BLUE TIT

FLAPPY FACT

The more of a certain type of caterpillar a blue tit eats, the stronger the yellow colour on its chest.

WRITE YOUR ANSWERS HERE:

1...

2...

3...

4...

ODD FLAPPY OUT

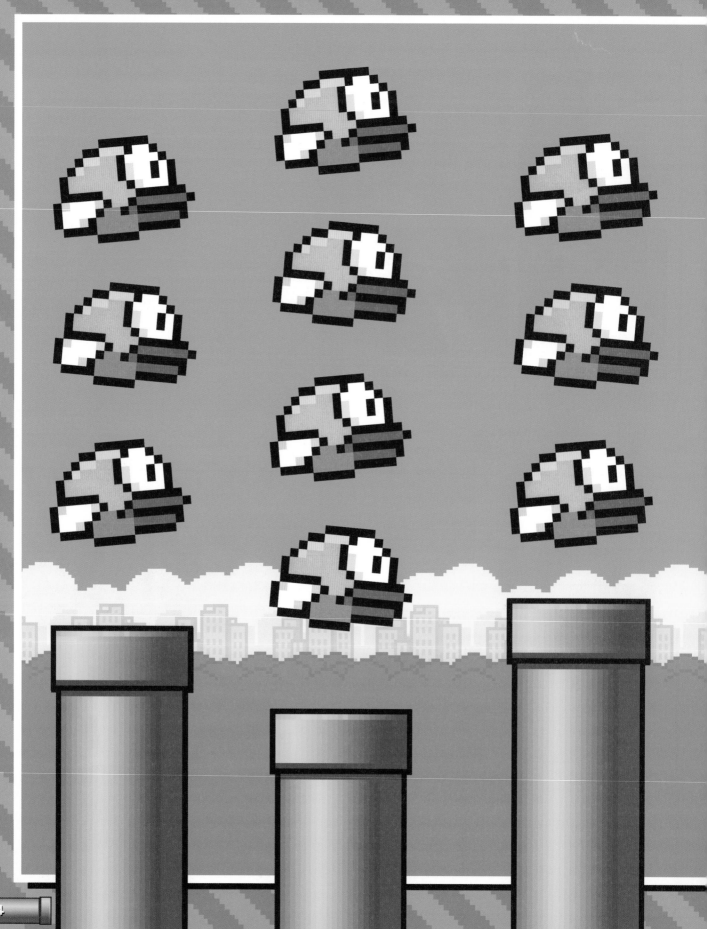

Look closely at Flappy Bird darting, dashing and diving. One of these Flappy's is different from the rest...Can you spot which one it is?

Flight paths

Each Flappy Bird flight path takes the fearless flyer on a different route to the finish. Use your finger to follow the paths and swoop, swoosh and sail across the page. Which bird makes it to the end without a splat attack?

FINISH

FINISH

Migrating Muddle

Many kinds of birds migrate every year, moving from one place to another in search of food and warmth. Flappy Bird wants to travel too, but the paths are in a tangle! Which track takes the birds to their new home?

NORTH

WEST

EAST

A B C D

FINISH SOUTH FINISH

Rattled Letters

Bouncing birds have knocked and rattled all these words into nonsense. Reorder the letters in the anagrams to make words about the game.

ladem...

pta..

ppei..

rdbi..

lcduo...

lxpei...

escro...

Bird  song

Birds make wonderful noises, from sweet melodies to crazy chattering. Rearrange the letters in the anagrams to make words that describe bird song.

clla...

ooth...

teewt...

sgni...

prihc...

illtr ....

Can you think of any other words to describe the sounds that birds make? Whistle while you think.

wbarel.........................

INGREDIENTS:

Honeydew Melon

Seedless Black Grapes

Small Watermelon

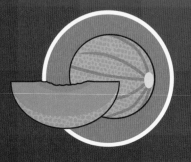

Cantaloupe Melon

Floppy Fruit salad

This is the funkiest, flappiest breakfast or snack. Assemble all the pixel pieces into a picture then eat your fruity art. This is a load of fun to create with friends that are fans of Flappy Bird! It's a melon masterpiece!

EQUIPTMENT:

- Chopping board - Kitchen knife - Large white plate

HOW TO MAKE:

STEP 1   Ask an adult to remove the skin and seeds from the melons and chop the fruit flesh into square chunks. Divide the melon colours into different bowls.

On a large plate, position melon pieces one by one to make an image of Flappy Bird. Use the picture to the right to help you. The red watermelon is for Flappy's mouth, the orange melon is for Flappy's tummy, and the yellow melon is for Flappy's body. Leave Flappy's wing and eye shapes empty so you can see the white plate.

STEP 3

Use the black grapes to outline the different areas and then place all around the edges of your melon bird.

FLAPPY FACT

Birds love to eat fruit, including cherries, apples, grapes, raspberries and blackberries.

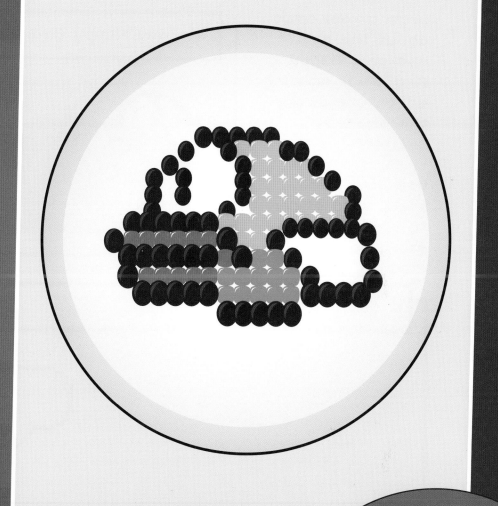

ASK AN ADULT TO PREPARE THE FRUIT. YOU MIGHT LIKE A LITTLE HELP WITH CONSTRUCTION TOO.

Comic Creator

Draw a cool comic about the one and only Flappy Bird. What amazing adventure awaits the awesome aviator?

Use your comic-style word stickers to complete each story panel.

One day Flappy Bird was...

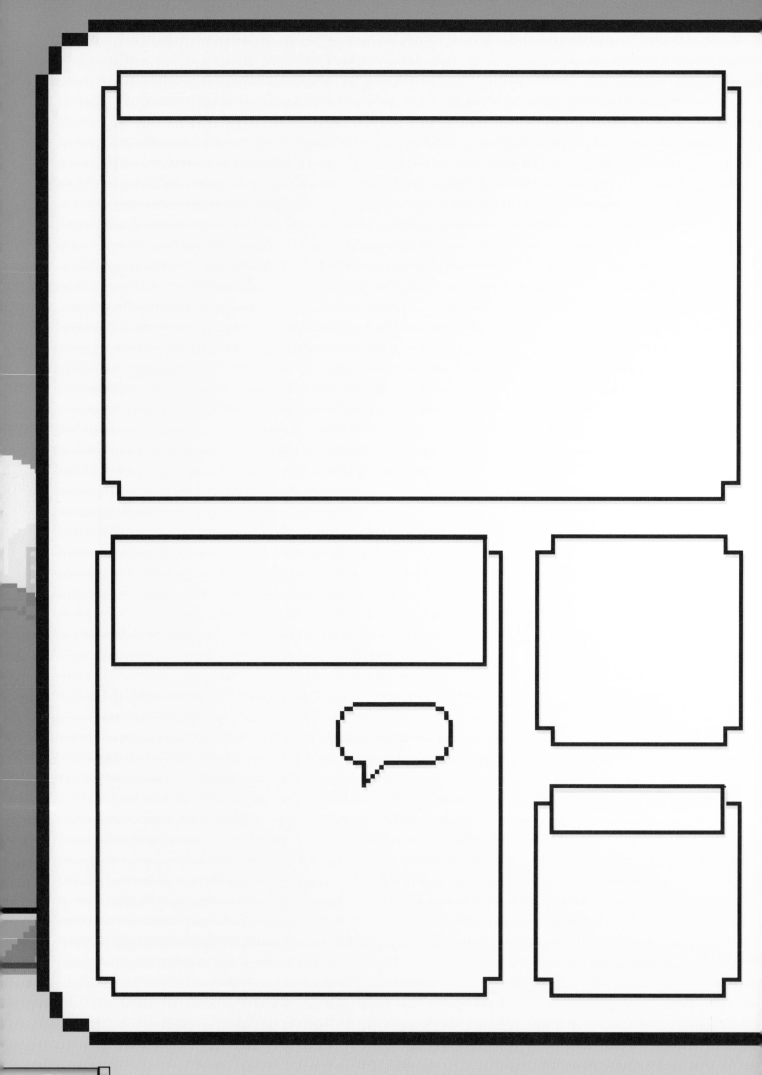

The End

WHERE IN THE WORLD IS FlappyBird?

Flappy Bird becomes snappy bird when he is exploring the world's tallest landmarks. Can you work out where he has been by matching up the photos he has snapped to the city names?

1

2

To help you, here are all of the places that Flappy Bird has visited.

NEPAL

RIO, BRAZIL

SYDNEY, AUSTRALIA

PISA, ITALY

GIZA, EGYPT

PARIS, FRANCE

LONDON, ENGLAND

NEW YORK, USA

3

4

5

6

7

8

MEDAL MAKER

- Tracing paper
- A4 white card
- Pencil
- Silver and gold colouring pens
- Scissors
- Long pieces of string or ribbon, or medium-sized safety pins
- Sticky tape

Medals are so shiny – they gleam with such a pleasing metal sheen. Getting a medal is Flappy Bird's only goal. It's what Flappy thinks about every day and this bird will bump into pipes and fly forever to get one! Now you and your friends can have the special medals!

MEDAL 1

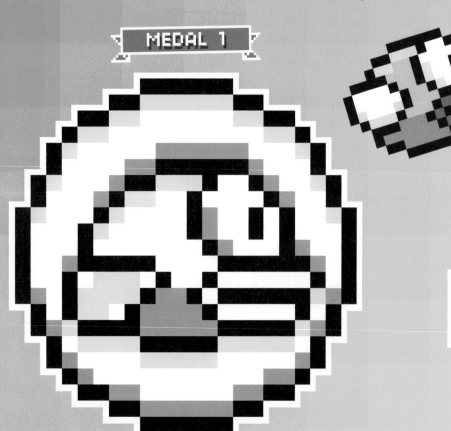

MEDAL 2

HOW TO MAKE:

STEP 1
Trace the medal art onto tracing paper and then the card. Repeat to make as many medals as you wish.

STEP 2
Colour the medals and cut out the card.

STEP 3
If you want to make a hanging medal, make a small hole in the top of the large medal. Cut a piece of string or ribbon long enough to loop loosely so that it hangs over your top. Thread the string or ribbon through the hole and knot the ends.

STEP 4
If you want to make medal badges, use sticky tape to attach safety pins to the back of the small-sized medal discs.

WEAR YOUR MEDALS WITH PRIDE AND HEAR FLAPPY BIRD FANS SING THEIR APPROVAL!

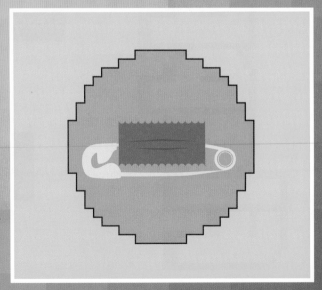

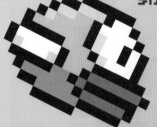

ASK AN ADULT TO HELP WITH CUTTING AND STICKING PINS.

Create a Look

STENCIL 1

1. cut out stencil 1 and 2 with a pair of scissors and place them on a white t-shirt.

2. Using special fabric coloured pens draw round the outline in black ink.

3. you can now use the coloured pens to brighten up the design on the t-shirt.

STENCIL 2

Sudoku Squawk

Help Flappy Bird finish the Sudoku challenge with stickers.

Each row and column must include all six pictures. Each 2 x 3 rectangle must also include six pictures.

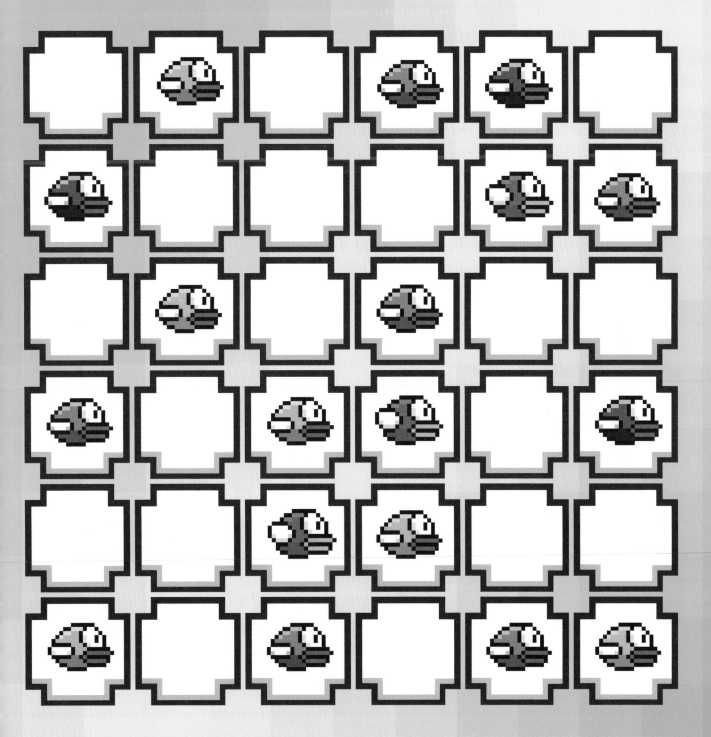

SQUAWK AS YOU STICK EACH SQUARE!

Birdie Jokes

Which jokes ruffle your feathers, make you giggle like a goose or hoot like an owl? Memorise these witty wisecracks to impress your friends!

Why do hummingbirds hum?
BECAUSE THEY FORGOT THE WORDS!

KNOCK KNOCK!
Who's there?
KOOK!
Kook who?
DON'T CALL ME CUCKOO!

What does a mixed-up hen lay?
SCRAMBLED EGGS!

What bird is helpful at dinner?
A SWALLOW!

What kind of bird can carry a big weight?
A CRANE!

What do you give a sick bird? TWEETMENT!

What do you get if you cross a canary and a long snake?
A SING-ALONG!

Who stole the soap?
THE ROBBER DUCKY!

What do you call an owl with a deep voice?
A GROWL!

KNOCK, KNOCK! Who's there? WHO. Who who? ARE YOU AN OWL?

How does a penguin build its house?
IGLOOS IT TOGETHER!

Where does a peacock go when it loses its tail?
A RETAIL STORE!

Flip over the page for more funnies!

What do you get if you cross a woodpecker with a carrier pigeon?
A BIRD THAT KNOCKS BEFORE DELIVERING A MESSAGE!

What do you get if you cross a centipede and a parrot?
A WALKIE-TALKIE!

How do crows stick together in a flock?
VEL-CROW!

What did one egg say to another egg?
LET'S GET CRACKIN'!

What do you call a seagull when it flies over a bay?
A BAGEL!

Where do birds meet for coffee?
IN A NEST-CAFE!

What do you call a bunch of turkeys playing hide and seek?
FOWL PLAY!

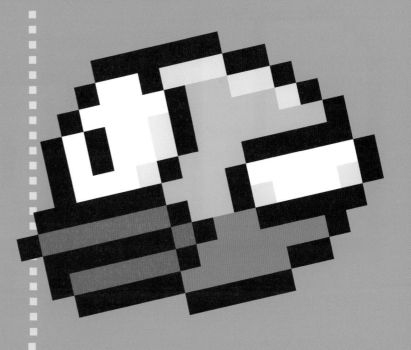

What happens when ducks fly upside down?
THEY QUACK UP!

Which bird is always out of breath?
A PUFFIN!

Why did the bird fly north?
BECAUSE IT WAS TOO FAR TO WALK!

Where do birds invest their money?
IN THE STORK MARKET!

What do you call a canary that flies into a pastry dish?
TWEETIE PIE!

Floppy Jokes

WHY DID FLAPPY FLY OVER THE ROAD? HOW MANY FUNNY ANSWERS TO THE JOKE QUESTION CAN YOU COME UP WITH?

Why did Flappy fly over the road? THERE WAS A CAR COMING!

Why did Flappy fly over the road? THE CHICKEN COULDN'T BE BOTHERED.

Get Ready!

WHY DID FLAPPY FLY OVER THE ROAD?

....

....

....

....

....

....

....

....

....

....

....

CHAMPION CHALLENGE

TIP 1

LOOK CLOSELY AT A BUSY SCENE AND FIND A SMALL OBJECT. SPIN AROUND TWICE AND TRY TO FIND THE SAME OBJECT AS SOON AS YOU STOP. CONCENTRATE THOSE EYES!

Are you ready for the ultimate Flappy Bird seven-day challenge? Check out the tweet-tastic training ideas, then turn the page to enter the competition zone and dare your fiends to take part in seven days of game battles. Who dares wins!

TIP 2
PRACTISE DRUMMING MORSE CODE WITH YOUR FINGER TO BUILD UP TAPPING STAMINA AND TAPPING RANGE.

TIP 3
USE A SMART PHONE OR TABLET DEVICE TO TAKE PICTURES OF BIRDS MOVING IN YOUR GARDEN. THE PRECISION NEEDED TO GET A GOOD PHOTO WILL HELP YOUR GAME SKILLS!

TIP 4
GET IN THE FLAPPY FRAME OF MIND. RUN AROUND, FLAPPING YOUR ARMS AND MAKING BIRD SOUNDS.

TIP 5
TEXT MESSAGE YOUR FRIENDS SEVERAL MESSAGES IN A ROW, AS FAST AS YOU CAN. THIS WILL HELP FINGER AGILITY.

TIP 6
HOLD YOUR SMART PHONE OR TABLET DEVICE IN DIFFERENT WAYS TO FIND THE BEST METHOD AND ANGLE FOR TOP TAPPING.

TIP 7
TRY PLAYING THE GAME AT DIFFERENT TIMES OF DAY TO SEE IF THAT CHANGES YOUR SCORING ABILITY.

TIP 8
TRY PLAYING THE GAME USING DIFFERENT FINGERS TO TAP. YOU MIGHT FIND YOUR BEST TAPPING FINGER IS NOT THE ONE YOU'VE BEEN USING!

TRAINING SCORES

Play the game three times in each battle. The person with the highest score from any game wins! Don't worry if you soar into pipes or skim along the ground. Keep your beak held high, bounce back in the air and flap again!

DAY 1	BATTLE 1	BATTLE 2	BATTLE 3
PLAYERS	.... VS.	.... VS.	.... VS. ....
SCORES			
WINNER			

DAY 2	BATTLE 1	BATTLE 2	BATTLE 3
PLAYERS	.... VS.	.... VS.	.... VS. ....
SCORES			
WINNER			

DAY 3	BATTLE 1	BATTLE 2	BATTLE 3
PLAYERS	.... VS.	.... VS.	.... VS. ....
SCORES	....	....	....
WINNER	....	....	....

DAY 4	BATTLE 1	BATTLE 2	BATTLE 3
PLAYERS	.... VS.	.... VS.	.... VS. ....
SCORES	....	....	....
WINNER	....	....	....

DAY 5	BATTLE 1	BATTLE 2	BATTLE 3
PLAYERS	.... VS.	.... VS.	.... VS. ....
SCORES	....	....	....
WINNER	....	....	....

DAY 6	BATTLE 1	BATTLE 2	BATTLE 3
PLAYERS	.... VS.	.... VS.	.... VS. ....
SCORES	....	....	....
WINNER	....	....	....

DAY 7	BATTLE 1	BATTLE 2	BATTLE 3
PLAYERS	.... VS.	.... VS.	.... VS. ....
SCORES	....	....	....
WINNER	....	....	....

MAKE-IT

Chocolate NESTS

Crunchy bird nests made of scrumptious syrupy chocolate? Yes, please and thank you!

INGREDIENTS:

50g Milk Chocolate Buttons

2Tbsp Cocoa Powder

2Tbsp Golden Syrup

100g Butter, Cubed

75g Cornflakes, Shredded Wheat or Puffed Rice Cereal

36 Mini Chocolate Eggs

EQUIPMENT:

- 12-hole cupcake tin - Cupcake cases
- 1 small saucepan or a microwave -
1 medium-sized bowl - Wooden spoon -
Kitchen scale

HOW TO MAKE:

STEP 1 Line the cupcake tin with paper cases.

Melt the chocolate, cocoa **STEP 2**
powder, golden syrup and
butter in a bowl set over a pan of
simmering water, (do not let the base
of the bowl touch the water).
Alternatively, heat the same ingredients
in a microwave on medium power until
melted. Stir the mixture until smooth

EXTRA NEST IDEAS:

- Roll thin tubes of marzipan to make worm decorations for your nests.
- Swap the cereal with a mixture of desiccated coconut, coconut flakes and almond flakes for a nutty nest!
- Melt a few marshmallows in the chocolate mixture to make really gooey nests.
- Swap cocoa powder with flavoured hot-chocolate powder such as mint, orange or caramel.
- Swap mini chocolate eggs with jellybeans to make nest eggs for tiny birds.

STEP 3

Remove the bowl from the heat and stir in the cereal (a few spoonfuls at a time), until it is completely coated in the chocolate mixture.

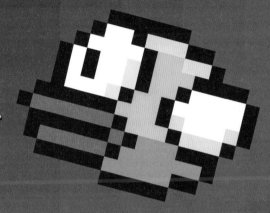

STEP 4

Divide the mixture between the paper cases. Use your fingers to make a shallow well in the centre of each nest and place inside 3 chocolate eggs. Chill in the fridge for 1 hour, or until set.

ASK AN ADULT TO MELT THE CHOCOLATE. YOUR JOB IS TO BUILD THE NESTS LIKE A BIRD!

Flappy patterns

Grab your bird-oculars and look closely at each sequence. Can you figure out what comes next in each row? Use your stickers for answers.

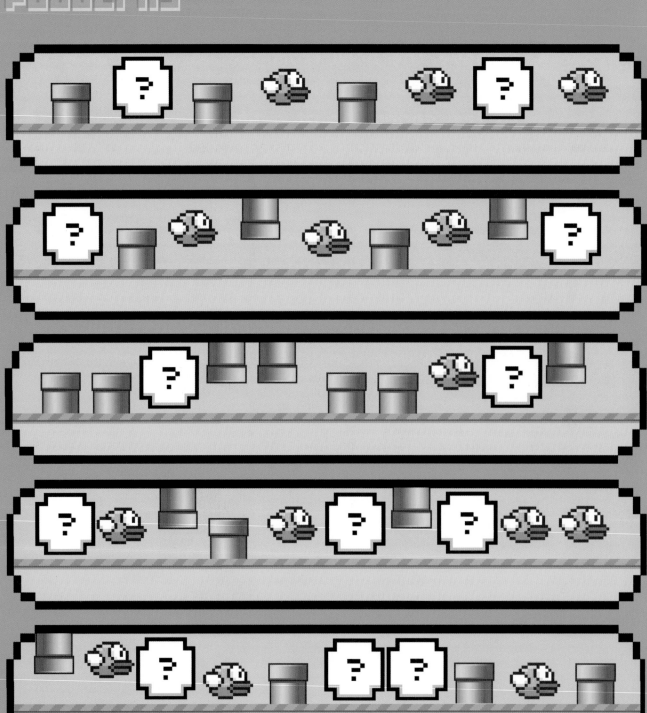

Game Glitch

Oops! Flappy's in a pixel pickle. Reorder the sections to make a correct picture of Flappy Bird. What do the letters spell?

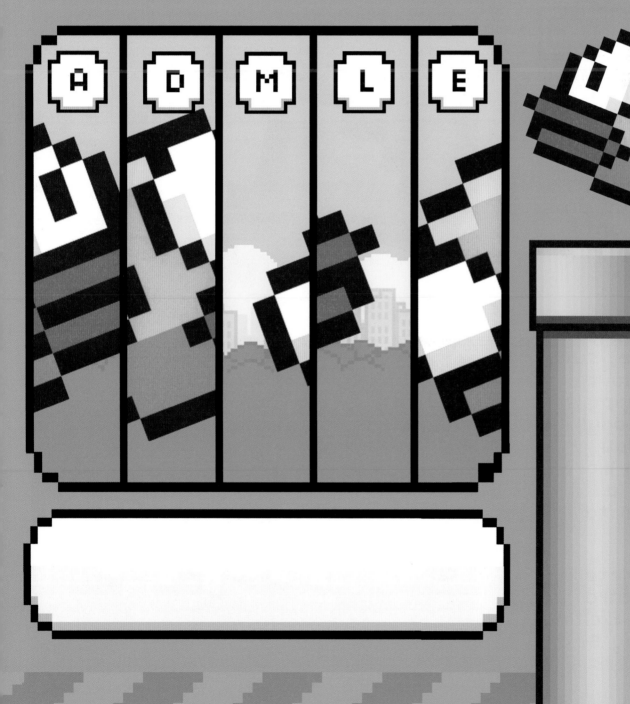

A D M L E

Bird-day Card Maker

Everyone loves to see post land on the doormat. Did you know that birds used to be trained as mail carriers? It was called pigeon post! Make a card for your friend, pop it in the post and imagine it flapping to their feet.

YOU WILL NEED:

- A scan or photocopy of opposite page
- A4 card, folded to A5 size
- Paper glue
- Scissors
- Pen or pencil

HOW TO MAKE:

1. Glue your chosen design to the card, placing it face up on the right side of the fold.

2. Add a message inside, such as 'Have a Flappy birthday!' or 'You mean more than a medal to me.'

3. Complete the card with exciting Flappy Bird stickers.

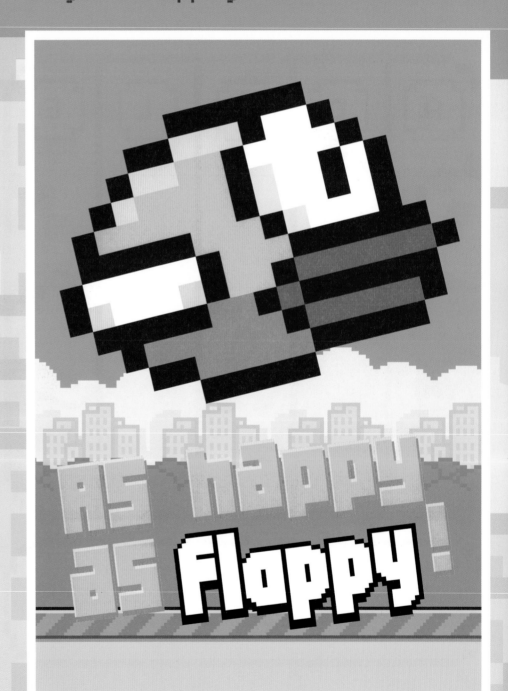

AS HAPPY AS Flappy

Flappy Bird-Day To You!
Flappy Bird-Day To You!

Pixel Post!

Just tweeting you to say...

ASK FOR HELP WITH CUTTING AND STICKING!

Wild Bird CHASE

CHASE 1

FINISH

Flappy Bird was playing a game of wild-bird chase when he got lost. Use your finger to tap along the path and guide your pixel pal back on track. If you find a dead end, flap backwards!

CHASE 2

Finders Keepers

Flappy is on a global quest for more medals. He'll flap to every corner of the world to find them! Can you spot a medal in each scene? Colour in a picture of Flappy when you find each medal.

MY FLAPPY YEAR!

JANUARY

T	F	S	S	M	T	W	T	F	S	S	M	T	W	T	F
1	2	3	4	5	6	7	8	9	10	11	12	13	14	15	16
S	S	M	T	W	T	F	S	S	M	T	W	T	F	S	
17	18	19	20	21	22	23	24	25	26	27	28	29	30	31	

FEBRUARY

S	M	T	W	T	F	S	S	M	T	W	T	F	S	S	M
1	2	3	4	5	6	7	8	9	10	11	12	13	14	15	16
T	W	T	F	S	S	M	T	W	T	F	S				
17	18	19	20	21	22	23	24	25	26	27	28				

MARCH

S	M	T	W	T	F	S	S	M	T	W	T	F	S	S	M
1	2	3	4	5	6	7	8	9	10	11	12	13	14	15	16
T	W	T	F	S	S	M	T	W	T	F	S	S	M	T	
17	18	19	20	21	22	23	24	25	26	27	28	29	30	31	

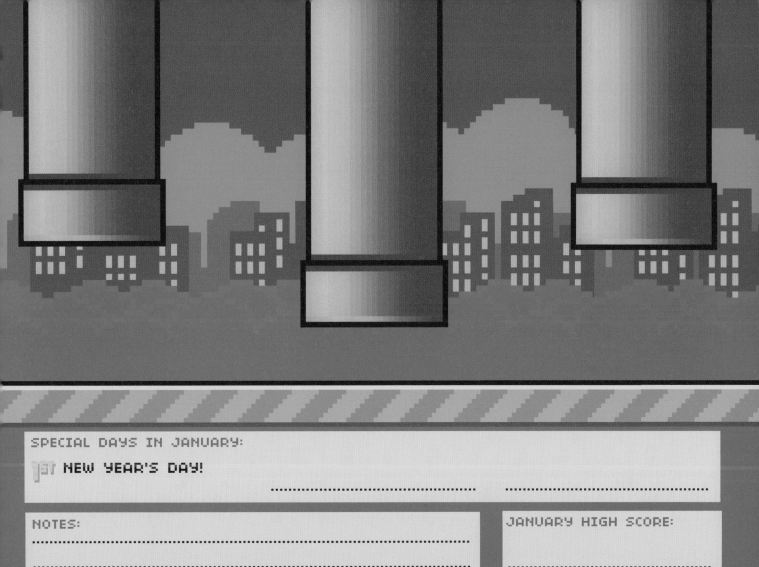

SPECIAL DAYS IN JANUARY:

1ST NEW YEAR'S DAY!

....

NOTES:

....
....

JANUARY HIGH SCORE:

....

SPECIAL DAYS IN FEBRUARY:

14TH VALENTINE'S DAY

....

NOTES:

....
....

FEBRUARY HIGH SCORE:

....

SPECIAL DAYS IN MARCH:

1ST ST DAVID'S DAY   **15TH MOTHER'S DAY**   **17TH ST PATRICK'S DAY**

NOTES:

....
....

MARCH HIGH SCORE:

....

APRIL

W	T	F	S	S	M	T	W	T	F	S	S	M	T	W	T
1	2	3	4	5	6	7	8	9	10	11	12	13	14	15	16
F	S	S	M	T	W	T	F	S	S	M	T	W	T		
17	18	19	20	21	22	23	24	25	26	27	28	29	30		

MAY

F	S	S	M	T	W	T	F	S	S	M	T	W	T	F	S
1	2	3	4	5	6	7	8	9	10	11	12	13	14	15	16
S	M	T	W	T	F	S	S	M	T	W	T	F	S	S	
17	18	19	20	21	22	23	24	25	26	27	28	29	30	31	

JUNE

M	T	W	T	F	S	S	M	T	W	T	F	S	S	M	T
1	2	3	4	5	6	7	8	9	10	11	12	13	14	15	16
W	T	F	S	S	M	T	W	T	F	S	S	M	T		
17	18	19	20	21	22	23	24	25	26	27	28	29	30		

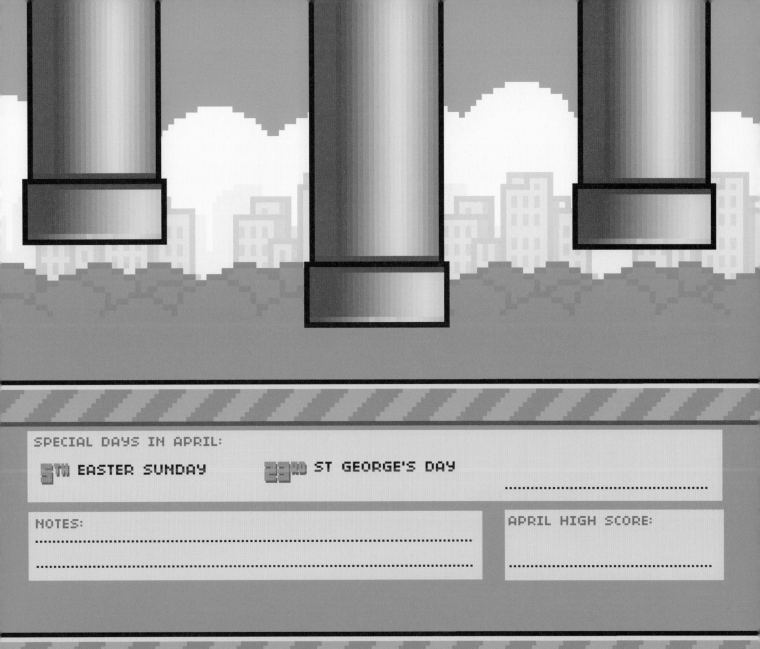

SPECIAL DAYS IN APRIL:

5TH EASTER SUNDAY   **23RD** ST GEORGE'S DAY

....

NOTES:

....

....

APRIL HIGH SCORE:

....

....

SPECIAL DAYS IN MAY:

4TH BANK HOLIDAY   **25TH** BANK HOLIDAY

....

NOTES:

....

....

MAY HIGH SCORE:

....

....

SPECIAL DAYS IN JUNE:

21ST FATHER'S DAY

....

NOTES:

....

....

JUNE HIGH SCORE:

....

....

JULY

W 1	T 2	F 3	S 4	S 5	M 6	T 7	W 8	T 9	F 10	S 11	S 12	M 13	T 14	W 15	T 16
F 17	S 18	S 19	M 20	T 21	W 22	T 23	F 24	S 25	S 26	M 27	T 28	W 29	T 30	F 31	

AUGUST

S 1	S 2	M 3	T 4	W 5	T 6	F 7	S 8	S 9	M 10	T 11	W 12	T 13	F 14	S 15	S 16
M 17	T 18	W 19	T 20	F 21	S 22	S 23	M 24	T 25	W 26	T 27	F 28	S 29	S 30	M 31	

SEPTEMBER

T 1	W 2	T 3	F 4	S 5	S 6	M 7	T 8	W 9	T 10	F 11	S 12	S 13	M 14	T 15	W 16
T 17	F 18	S 19	S 20	M 21	T 22	W 23	T 24	F 25	S 26	S 27	M 28	T 29	W 30		

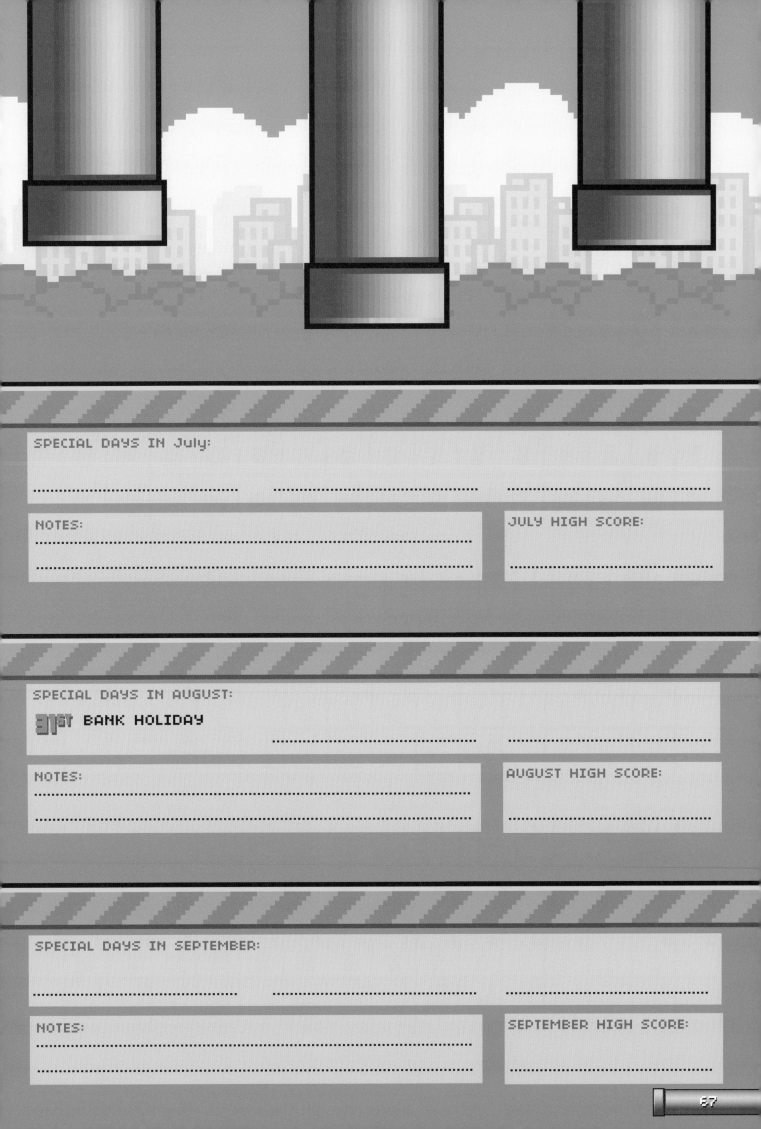

SPECIAL DAYS IN July:

....

NOTES:

....

....

JULY HIGH SCORE:

....

SPECIAL DAYS IN AUGUST:

31ST BANK HOLIDAY

....

NOTES:

....

....

AUGUST HIGH SCORE:

....

SPECIAL DAYS IN SEPTEMBER:

....

NOTES:

....

....

SEPTEMBER HIGH SCORE:

....

october

T	F	S	S	M	T	W	T	F	S	S	M	T	W	T	F
1	2	3	4	5	6	7	8	9	10	11	12	13	14	15	16
S	S	M	T	W	T	F	S	S	M	T	W	T	F	S	
17	18	19	20	21	22	23	24	25	26	27	28	29	30	31	

NOVEMBER

S	M	T	W	T	F	S	S	M	T	W	T	F	S	S	M
1	2	3	4	5	6	7	8	9	10	11	12	13	14	15	16
T	W	T	F	S	S	M	T	W	T	F	S	S	M		
17	18	19	20	21	22	23	24	25	26	27	28	29	30		

DECEMBER

T	W	T	F	S	S	M	T	W	T	F	S	S	M	T	W
1	2	3	4	5	6	7	8	9	10	11	12	13	14	15	16
T	F	S	S	M	T	W	T	F	S	S	M	T	W	T	
17	18	19	20	21	22	23	24	25	26	27	28	29	30	31	

SPECIAL DAYS IN OCTOBER:

31ST HALLOWEEN

....

NOTES:

....
....

OCTOBER HIGH SCORE:

....

SPECIAL DAYS IN NOVEMBER:

5TH GUY FAWKES NIGHT   11TH REMEMBRANCE DAY   30TH ST ANDREW'S DAY

NOTES:

....
....

NOVEMBER HIGH SCORE:

....

SPECIAL DAYS IN DECEMEBER:

25TH CHRISTMAS DAY   26TH BOXING DAY   31ST NEW YEAR'S EVE

NOTES:

....
....

DECEMEBER HIGH SCORE:

....

Birding About

Flappy Bird is looking through his favourite summer holiday photographs. Where did he go?

Flappy's stuck in a tree! What else is stuck up there with him?

It's Easter and Flappy Bird has decorated Easter eggs for all his friends. Can you decide which one looks the best?

1

2

3

Feathered friends!
Flappy's meeting birds
of paradise in the
jungle. Sketch some
ideas for exotic birds
never seen before.

Baby Birds

Flappy Bird thinks little fledglings are so fluffy and floppy, and their tiny tweets are really sweet! Can you match each picture of a nest-warm chick to a picture of a proud parent?

TWEET TWOOO

SQUAWK

Blue jay

Duck

Toucan

Swan

Owl

FLAPPY FACT

A baby owl is called an owlet, a baby duck is called a duckling, a baby swan is called a cygnet and a baby dove is called a squab.

Look out for cute baby birds in springtime, but be careful not to disturb them.

Emu

Peacock

Kestrel

CLUCK and COO as YOU match!

Three birds have stepped in wet paint and flapped all over the place! Use your finger to tap along the brightly coloured footprints. How many medals has each bird pecked?

MONEY BOX MAKER

Keep all your pennies in a safe box!

YOU WILL NEED:

- A scan or photocopy of the opposite page
- A4 card
- Paper glue
- Scissors
- Ruler (optional)
- Colouring pens or pencils

HOW TO MAKE:

STEP 1 Glue the copy of the box template onto card.

STEP 2 Cut out the template along the blue lines.

STEP 3 Use the ruler and scissors to score along the dotted lines. Fold the tabs inwards.

STEP 4 Cut a slot hole where it says "Get Ready!"

STEP 5 Glue the tabs and fold the template into a box shape, pressing the pieces that meet the tabs to stick them together.

STEP 6 Save your pennies!

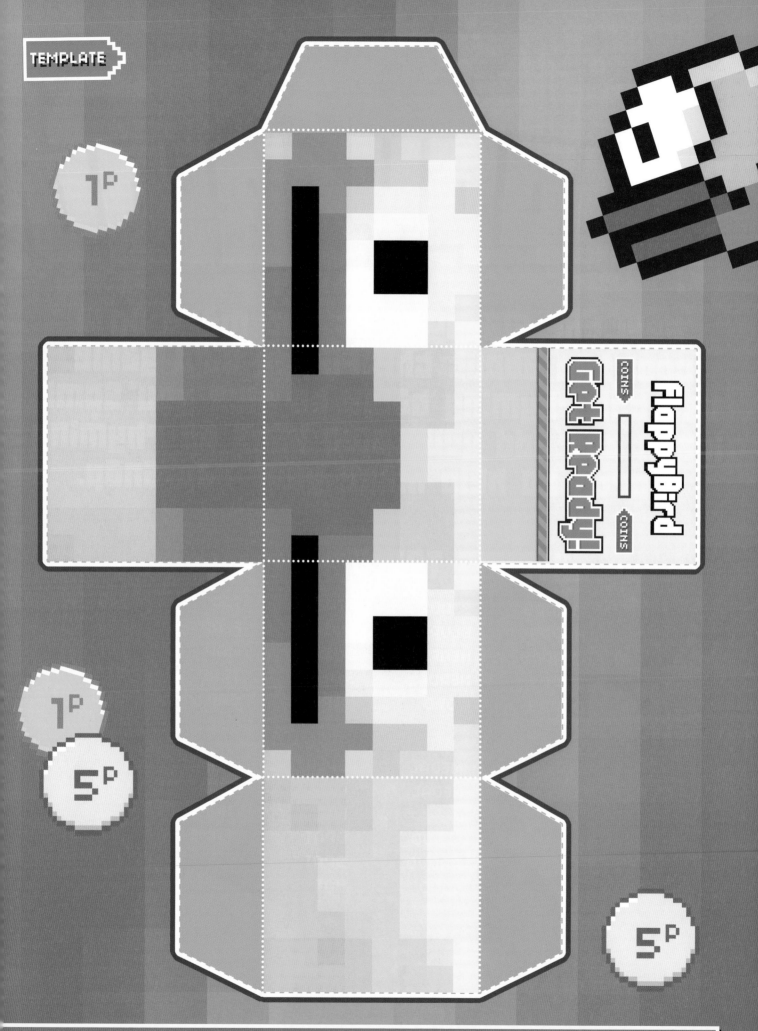

TEMPLATE

1P

1P

5P

5P

FlappyBird

COINS

COINS

Get Ready!

ASK AN ADULT TO HELP YOU CUT AND SCORE.

RAPPY BIRD

Feel the Flappy beat and make up a cool rap about the Flappy Bird game. Use the rhyming table to give you some ideas and add your own lists of rhyming words to help make your rap snap.

RHYMING TABLE

FLAPPY	BIRD	PIPE	TAP	FLY
HAPPY	BLURRED	SWIPE	FLAP	TRY
CHAPPY	HEARD	SNIPE	MAP	WHY
SAPPY	NERD	STRIPE	TRAP	SIGH
DAPPY	WORD	WIPE	GAP	SKY

	MEDAL	SPLAT	GAME
	PEDAL	CAT	AIM
		FAT	NAME
		DRAT	FAME
	CLOUD	SPAT	
	PROUD	HAT	
	LOUD		

YOUR RAP GOES HERE!

FLAPPY FACTS

Twit twoo as you think about these bird-flight facts.

Alpine swifts have the longest recorded flight time in history!

SOARING BIRDS KEEP IN THE AIR WITHOUT FLAPPING BY LOCKING SPECIAL TENDONS IN THEIR WINGS.

When in a hunting dive, the peregrine falcon can reach speeds of 200mph.

THE TWO FEATURES THAT LET BIRDS FLY ARE WINGS AND FEATHERS. SIMPLE AS THAT.

Wandering albatrosses have the largest wingspan of any living bird.

THE WORLD'S HIGHEST-FLAPPING BIRDS ARE BAR-HEADED GEESE.

Woodcocks like to take their time – they have the slowest flight patterns.

THE HEAVIEST FLYING BIRD IS THE GREAT BUSTARD – IT CAN WEIGH AROUND THE SAME AMOUNT AS A FIVE-YEAR-OLD HUMAN CHILD.

Hummingbirds can flap their wings faster than any other bird.

MEDAL TALLY

Flappy Bird has collected more medals than ever before! It's a heavy haul for the little featherweight flap star! How many gold, silver and bronze medals can you count?

YOU HAD BETTER WATCH OUT FOR FAKE MEDALS!

Flappy Bird has collected:

.... GOLD MEDALS

.... SILVER MEDALS

.... BRONZE MEDALS

& .... FAKES

HINT: YOU CAN TELL A FAKE BY LOOKING INTO FLAPPY'S EYES.

MAKE-IT MASK

When you wear this mask you will magically become Flappy Bird! Watch out for the pipes when you go hunting for medals!

YOU WILL NEED:

- Tracing paper
- A4 white card
- Pencil
- Colouring pens
- Scissors
- 2 long pieces of string or ribbon

HOW TO MAKE:

STEP 1 Trace the mask lines onto the tracing paper and then the card.

STEP 2 Colour the mask and cut out the card along the edge of the design.

STEP 3 Pierce a hole through each side and cut out the eye shapes along the dashed lines.

STEP 4 Thread the string through the holes and knot the ends so that they can't pass back through. Align the mask with your eyes and tie the string in a bow at the back of your head.

FLAPPY FACT

Most birds have patterned feathers to help hide in their surroundings. The reed-dwelling bittern is so well masked by its reed-patterned body that it's rarely seen.

MAKER

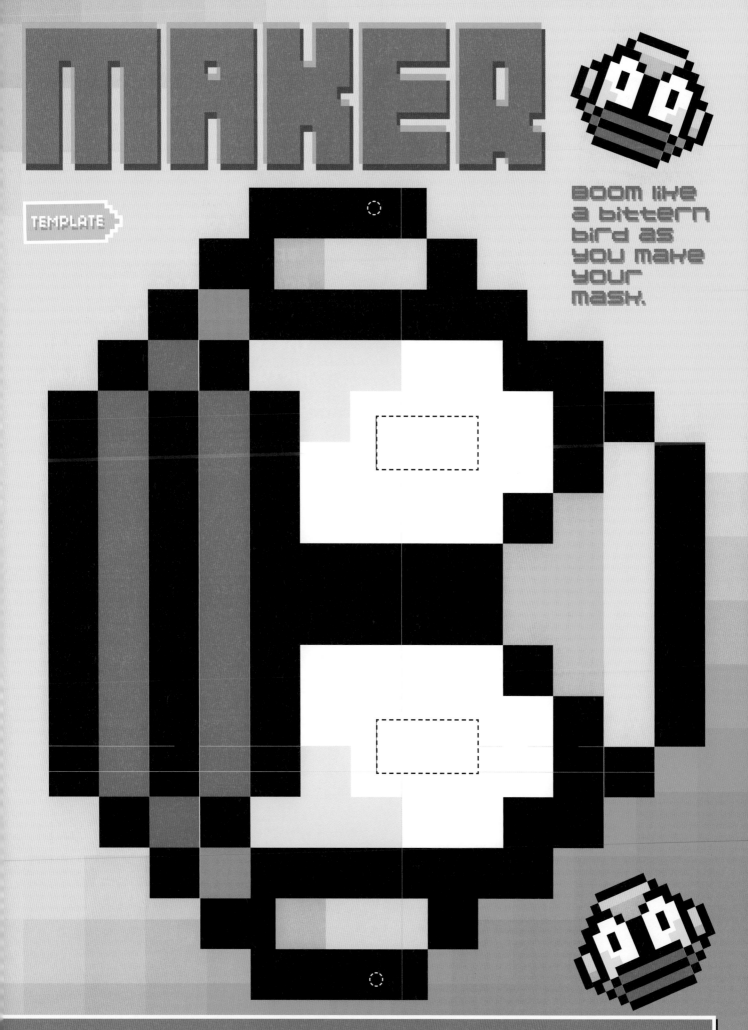

TEMPLATE

BOOM like a bittern bird as you make your mask.

ASK AN ADULT TO HELP, ESPECIALLY WITH CUTTING, HOLE MAKING AND TYING.

85

SHATTERED SCREENS

Uh-oh! Lots of tempered tapping has made these game screens crack! Link the screen pieces to the correct places in the picture so that it's not game over.

TRUE OR FALSE

Bird facts can be so incredible - it's hard to know what is true and what is a flight of fancy. Can you help Flappy Bird guess which statements are true and which are false? Here's a tip - five are false.

1. Spider stuffing!

A house wren can feed 500 spiders and caterpillars to its babies during a single summer afternoon.

TRUE ☐ FALSE ☐

2. Sonic searcher!

An owl can hear a mouse treading on a twig 100 metres away.

TRUE ☐ FALSE ☐

3. Venus fly trap!

A tawny frogmouth waits for a frog or small bird to come close before it opens its large mouth to scoop up the snack and click its beak shut.

TRUE ☐ FALSE ☐

4. Vulture vomit!

When danger threatens, a turkey vulture defends itself by puking up its last meal.

TRUE ☐ FALSE ☐

5. Superhero strength!

A harpy eagle has crushing strength greater than the jaws of a tiger.

TRUE ☐ FALSE ☐

6. Fast food!

Roadrunners run as fast as Olympic sprinters to catch food such as lizards, snakes, rodents, scorpions and tarantulas.

TRUE ☐ FALSE ☐

7. Daredevil diver!
A gannet bird dives into the sea at speeds up to 150mph, using its helmet-like skull to protect it.

TRUE ☐ FALSE ☐

TRUE ☐ FALSE ☐

8. World domination!
At any given time, there are between one and two billion living birds on the planet.

9. Pre-historic family tree!
Some scientists believe that the ostrich is directly related to the Tyrannosaurus rex.

TRUE ☐ FALSE ☐

10. Clever fishers!
Just like humans, green herons use hooked bait to catch fish.

TRUE ☐ FALSE ☐

11. Song sensation!
Lyrebirds can mimic any sound perfectly, including voices, music and machines.

TRUE ☐ FALSE ☐

12. Yolk yikes!
15 yolks have been found in one chicken egg.

TRUE ☐ FALSE ☐

13. Old giant!
The now extinct Madagascan elephant bird got its name because it was as big as an elephant.

TRUE ☐ FALSE ☐

14. As light as a feather?
A bird's feathers weigh more than its skeleton does.

TRUE ☐ FALSE ☐

15. Run-away teen!
Some nestling storks have been seen to run away from home and sneak into another family nest in the hope for better food.

TRUE ☐ FALSE ☐

Flappy CAKES

Make these cakes for a party to celebrate with Flappy style.

INGREDIENTS:

MAKES 10

CAKE SPONGE

100g Caster Sugar

100g Butter, Softened

2 Eggs

100g Self-Raising Flour

1Tbsp Milk

THE FILLING

50g Butter, Softened

75g Icing Sugar

2Tbsp Jam

TO FINISH

Icing Sugar, For Dusting

EQUIPMENT:

- Muffin/cupcake tray

- Paper muffin/ cupcake cases

- Wooden spoon

- Large bowl

- Medium bowl

- Sieve

- Wire cooling rack

- Chopping board and knife

- Teaspoon

STEP 1 Preheat the oven to 190°C/Gas Mark 5. Line a muffin tray with 10 paper muffin cases.

STEP 2 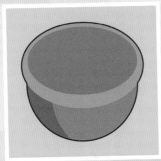 Place the sugar, butter, eggs, flour and milk in the large bowl and beat with the wooden spoon until the mixture is a pale and creamy batter.

STEP 3 Divide the mixture between the muffin cases and bake for 15-20 minutes until risen, golden and firm to the touch. Transfer to the wire rack and leave to cool.

STEP 4 To make the buttercream, place the butter in the medium-sized bowl and sift over the icing sugar. Clean the wooden spoon and use it to beat the buttercream until smooth.

STEP 5 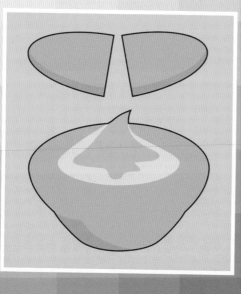 Slice the top off each cake and fill the centres with a teaspoon of buttercream and jam. Cut each sliced top in half and arrange on top of the filling to resemble bird wings. Dust lightly with icing sugar.

YOU'LL NEED AN ADULT TO HELP YOU MAKE THESE CAKES.

MEMORY GAME

Does your mind flit and fleet between thoughts? Concentrate on this game picture for thirty seconds and look at everything, remembering as much detail as possible. Then cover the scene and see if you can answer the questions on the opposite page.

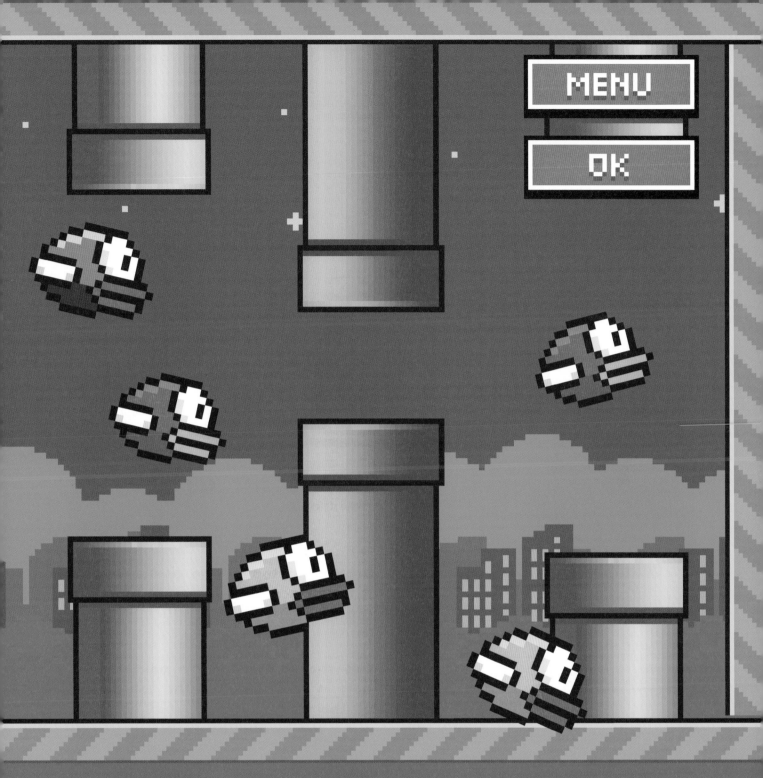

MENU

OK

1. How many orange birds are in the flappy picture?

....

2. How many blue birds are in the flappy picture?

....

3. How many green birds are in the flappy picture?

....

4. Are there more green than brown pipes?

....

5. Is it night or day for Flappy Bird?

....

6. Have any birds crashed into any pipes? (if so, how many?)

....

7. Which side of the image has more birds?

....

8. What is the colour of the bird flying in the wrong directon?

....

9. How many birds are there all together in this image?

....

Build a Birdhouse

- Old newspaper
- Large juice carton, clean and dried
- Stapler
- Ruler
- Marker pen
- Scissors
- Screwdriver
- Unsharpened pencil
- Quick-dry strong glue
- Masking tape
- Brown shoe polish
- Old cloth
- Long length of twine

Every bird needs a cosy nest for snuggles and snoozing. Why not build a den to tempt travelling birds looking for a home in your neighbourhood? This birdhouse is the perfect size for small garden birds.

HOW TO MAKE:

STEP 1 Cover your work area with the old newspaper.

STEP 2 Staple the top of the carton shut or if it has a screw-top opening, screw the cap on tight.

STEP 3

Use the screwdriver to make a hole in the middle of the top edge of the carton. This is what you will hang the birdhouse from.

STEP 4 Draw a 3cm-wide circle 15cm up from the bottom of the carton. Cut out the hole. This will be the entry hole for the birds.

STEP 5 Roughly 2cm below the entry hole, make a small, pencil-sized hole in the same place on the front and back of the carton.

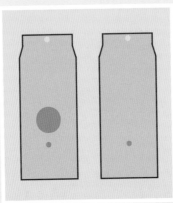

Turn the carton over and make four small holes in the bottom side for drainage.

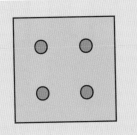

STEP 7 Now to decorate the birdhouse! Cover the carton with horizontal strips of masking tape (being careful not to cover the holes). Overlap the tape and use different lengths to make it look uneven. Use the old cloth to dab brown shoe polish onto the tape to make it look like wooden slats. Leave to dry.

STEP 8

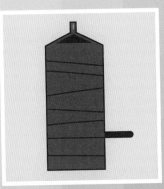

Insert the pencil into the small hole beneath the entry circle, pushing the pencil through so that a 3cm ledge sticks out at the front. Use a little glue to stick the pencil in place. Allow the glue to dry.

STEP 9 Thread a piece of twine through the hole in the top of the carton and tie the ends to create a loop so that it can be hung from a tree or nail.

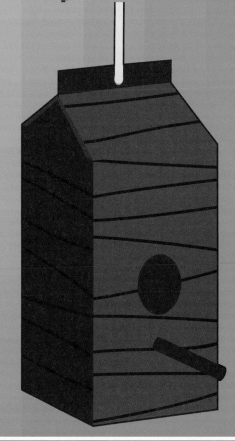

STEP 10 Thread a piece of twine through the hole in the top of the carton and tie the ends to create a loop so that it can be hung from a tree or nail.

ASK AN ADULT TO HELP YOU WITH HOLE MAKING, CUTTING, GLUING AND TYING.

FLAPPY SCHOOL

Help Flappy Bird figure out the answers to these tricky questions. Babble and beep like a bird to help you think.

1. Flappy Bird flies past 20 pipes. He hits 8 pipes along the way. How many pipes does Flappy Bird successfully fly through?

2. Flappy Bird has collected 6 gold medals, 3 silver medals and 10 bronze medals. How many medals does he have in total?

3. If you play 15 games and lose 6, how many games have you won?

4. If you tap your finger twice every second and 7 seconds pass, how many times have you tapped your finger?

5. Flappy Bird flaps 10 times in between clouds. How many times does he flap after 4 clouds?

6. Flappy Bird meets 5 blue birds, 4 red birds and 7 yellow birds. How many birds does Flappy meet altogether?

YOU CAN DO YOUR WORKING OUT HERE!

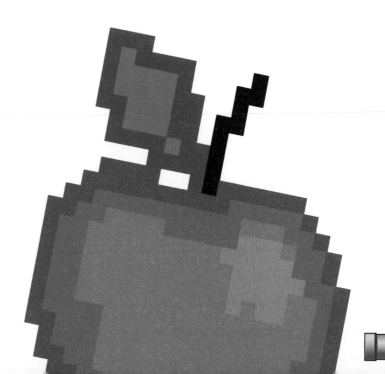

MAKE-IT

egg Experiment

WHAT YOU NEED:

4 Clear Plastic Cups

4 eggs

WHITE VINEGAR

1 bottle of white vinegar

Eggs don't bounce like Flappy Bird! Or do they? Round up three flappy friends and try this experiment to find out how you can transform eggs that break into eggs that bounce!

HOW TO MAKE:

STEP 1

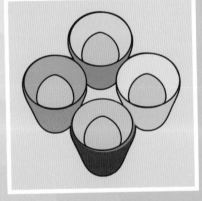

Carefully place one egg in each cup.

STEP 2 Fill the cups with vinegar until the eggs are covered with liquid.

STEP 3 ▸ Leave the eggs in a cupboard for four days.

STEP 4 ▸ Pour out the vinegar and rinse the eggs in water. Pat dry.

STEP 5 ▸ Gather your friends at a table and ask everyone to hold an egg in their hand. Lift your arm up about 30cm from the tabletop and let the egg drop to the table.

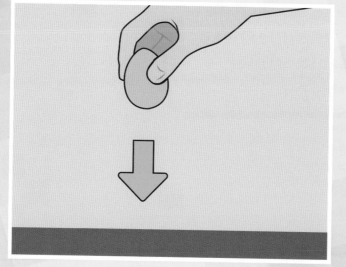

STEP 6 ▸ Create a contest to see who has the egg that can bounce from the highest point.

BOUNCE-O-METER

OSTRICH EGG

EMU EGG

GOOSE EGG

DUCK EGG

CHICKEN EGG

PHEASANT EGG

QUAIL EGG

YOU SHOULD GO OUTSIDE TO BOUNCE YOUR EGGS – THEY COULD MAKE A HUGE MESS!

Birding About

Super friends! Draw superhero Flappy Bird and his super side-kick friend.

Lazy Flappy Bird has decided to try a new mode of transport! Draw what this could be... (HINT: It's full of hot air!)

Bizarre and bulbous! What's blocking the pipes?

Cloud dreams! What pictures can you see in the clouds?

Flappy

FLOCK MOBILE MAKER

WHAT YOU NEED:

- TRACING PAPER
- A4 WHITE CARD
- PENCIL
- TISSUE PAPER IN DIFFERENT COLOURS, SUGGEST RED, BLUE, ORANGE
- QUICK-DRY PAPER GLUE
- SCISSORS
- DIFFERENT LENGTHS OF GREEN OR ORANGE RIBBON
- DIFFERENT LENGTHS OF STRING
- COLOUR CRAFT FEATHERS (OPTIONAL)
- STICKY TAPE
- 2 WIRE COAT HANGERS

Try making this floating bird mobile to create a flock of Flappy Birds for your room.

HOW TO MAKE:

STEP 1 — Trace the mobile pieces onto the tracing paper and then the card. Repeat to make as many mobile pieces as you wish.

STEP 2 — Pierce a hole through the mark on each piece.

STEP 3 — Tear strips off the tissue paper and scrunch them into small balls. One at a time glue the balls onto the card pieces, building up areas of colour to match the game art. Be careful not to cover the holes with tissue paper. When one side is dry, turn the card over and decorate the other side with tissue-paper balls in the same way.

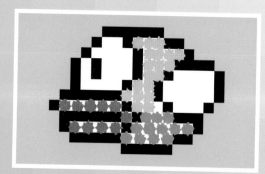

STEP 4 — Cut out the tissue-paper covered mobile pieces.

STEP 5 — Slot the wire hangers together at right angles and fix with sticky tape.

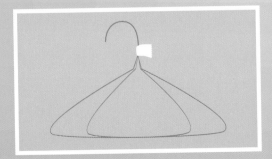

STEP 6

Thread a length of string through a mobile piece and knot the end to stop it passing through the hole. Tie the other end of the string to the hanger. Repeat with the other mobile pieces.

STEP 7

Tie the mobile pieces evenly along the wire hangers. Tie lengths of ribbon in between the mobile pieces. The ribbons will look like the pipes from the game!

STEP 8

If you are using craft feathers, stick or hang them wherever there is a gap on the wire frame.

STEP 9

Hang your mobile from a hook in the ceiling.

FLAPPY FACT

Red-billed queleas are a kind of weaver bird and form huge flocks which can include thousands of birds.

Honk and gaggle like a goose as you make the game-inspired mobile.

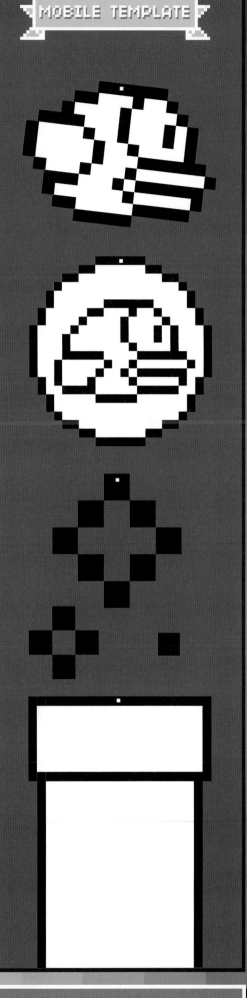

ASK AN ADULT TO HELP WITH MAKING HOLES AND CUTTING CARD.

PIXEL Bird DROPPINGS

Flappy Bird's been on a tour of famous landmarks in the UK. You can tell by the pixel bird droppings! See around the splats and guess where the fast-moving critter has flown.

1

2

To help you, here are the places that Flappy has visited.

London Eye

Blackpool Tower

Edinburgh Castle

Stonehenge

White Cliffs of Dover

Angel of the North

Roman Baths

Snowdonia Mountains

3

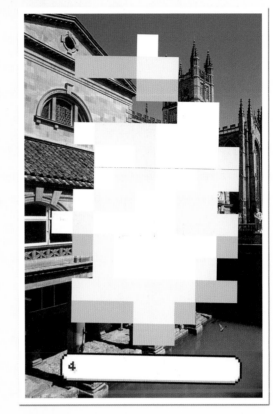

4

5

6

7

8

World Bird Map

There are way too many types of birds in the world to fit on one page, but here is a special selection to peck your interest and make you flap your way to a bird encyclopedia!

NORTH AMERICA 1

CENTRAL AMERICA 2

SOUTH AMERICA 3

EUROPE 4

MIDDLE EAST 6

ASIA 5

AFRICA 7

AUSTRALIA 8

1

BLUE JAY

A bright and social creature which forms tight family bonds. Its fondness for acorns helped spread oak trees over a huge area.

2

QUETZAL

This stunning bird was sacred to the ancient Maya and Aztec people. Royalty and priests wore its feathers during ceremonies.

3

SCARLET IBIS

The bright red plumage of this wading bird intensifies as it grows older. The colour comes from the crustaceans that it eats.

4

HOOPOE

A bird with a pretty crown on its head that opens when it is excited or surprised. It's named after the noise of its call: oop-oop-oop.

5

BAR-TAILED TREECREEPER

Flecked and striped feather patterns let this little mouse-like bird blend into the colours of the bark on the trees.

6

PALESTINE SUNBIRD

This black bird shines with colour when it moves in sunlight. It has a high, fast jingling call.

7

LOVEBIRDS

Lovebirds mate for life. Fossils of ancient lovebird species have been unearthed in South Africa dating to as far back as 1.9 million years ago.

8

KOOKABURRA

A type of kingfisher that has a laughter-like call. This tree bird gets all the moisture it needs from food, so it never needs to drink water.

PIXEL ART

WHAT YOU NEED:

- OLD NEWSPAPER
- LARGE POTATOES
- SHARP KNIFE
- PEN OR PENCIL
- POSTER PAINTS
- SHALLOW DISHES
- PAPER

Homemade art makes the perfect present for family and friends. Here's a great way to make pixel posters!

HOW TO MAKE:

STEP 1   Cover your work area with the old newspaper.

STEP 2   Wash the potatoes to remove any dirt.

You could cut loads of different sized squares to give extra detail to your poster!

STEP 3 Cut each potato in half. Draw or trace a square to use as your stamp onto the potato.

STEP 4 Cut around the square you drew, making cuts approx. 2cm deep.

STEP 5 Slice from the side of the potato about 2cm from the edge, cutting towards your stamp design, but being careful not to cut into it. Repeat on the different sides of the potato, until your stamp design protrudes out from the potato face.

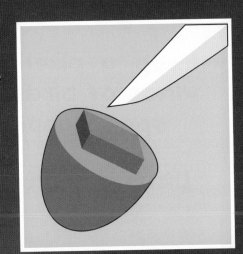

STEP 6 Pour paint into a shallow dish. Dip the potato stamp into the paint and press against the paper.

STEP 7 To use a different colour, rinse the potato and pat dry before dipping it into another paint dish.

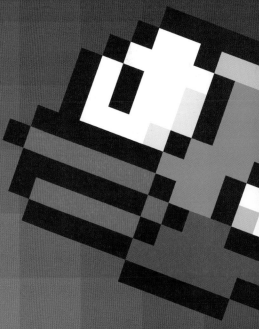

ASK AN ADULT TO CUT THE POTATOES FOR YOU.

BIRD WATCHING

Keep a pixel eye out for all the different kinds of birds in your area. Record what you spot flapping around and chirping here.

DATE:	FLAPPY BIRD:	NO. SPOTTED:

FlappyBird

Sticker Scene

Recreate a scene
from the amazing
Flappy Bird game
with your stickers.

UP, UP, UP

Play these fun ping-pong ball competitions with your flap-loving friends to help you get better at the Flappy Bird game.

YOU WILL NEED:

Ping-pong balls
Big cardboard box lid
Paper/plastic cups
Sticky tape
Scissors
Drinking straws

HAZARD MAZE

- Pick up the big, cardboard box lid. Cut several holes in it, big enough for the ping-pong ball to fit through easily. Place a ping-pong ball at one end of the box lid. Take turns tipping and turning the lid to try and move the ball around the holes and get it to the other side of the box.

- To change the game, tape a paper/plastic cup to the bottom of the box under one of the holes. Try to avoid all the holes except this one. If you get the ball in the cup without letting it fall through any of the other holes, you win!

PING-PONG BALL RACES

- You need at least four players, each with a straw. Stand around a table, with one person at each side. Put a ping-pong ball in the middle of the table.

- One player shouts "Go!" The idea is to use the straw to blow the ball off someone else's side of the table, while protecting your own side.

THE HOVERING PING-PONG BALL

- Bend a flexible straw so the short end is sticking straight up. With scissors, cut a fringe into the end of the straw, not quite to the bend. Bend out each piece of the fringe to create a cradle for a ping pong ball to sit in and pop a ball in place. Blow on the other end of the straw to make it hover. Once everyone has a straw and ball ready, start a competition to see who can make their ball hover the longest, or who can walk the farthest while making their ball hover.

PING-PONG CUP

- Arrange large paper cups in rows of 3-2-1 at one end of a table. Stand at the opposite end of the table with a ping-pong ball. Take turns to try and bounce the ball into a cup. Once you get a ball in a cup, take the cup away and try and score another cup. The winner is the person who takes the most cups.

EGG-CELLENT!

There are so many ways to decorate eggs. Ask an adult to help. Hard-boil a set of six white eggs for ten minutes and wait for them to cool a little. Now gather your craft material and get arty! Here are a few nuggets of ideas to create a colourful nest of eggs.

DYED RICE.

While you wait for the egg to cool completely, dye some rice.

1. Put rice, food colouring, water and parchment paper in a plastic bag and leave for 30 minutes.

2. Drain the bag and scatter the rice on a tray. Bake in a hot oven for a short while to dry the rice. Set aside until cold.

3. Cover the cold egg with glue and roll in the dyed rice.

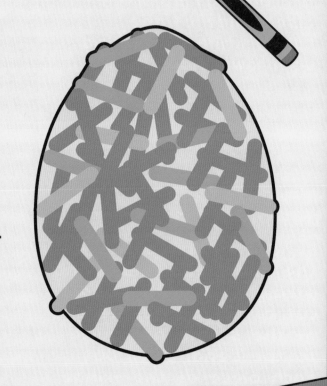

WAX CRAYONS.
Residual heat from the still-warm eggs will melt the wax so you don't have to press too hard.

STICKERS AND FELT-TIP PENS.
Draw and stick to your heart's content! You might have to go over your drawn design again to make the colours brighter.

TIE-DYE.

1. Find an old tie that is 100% silk.

2. Open the seams and cut a section of fabric that can wrap around your egg, plus an extra 6cm. Wrap the egg with the right side of the material touching the eggshell and secure tightly with a twisty-tie.

3. Wrap the egg with a second layer of plain cotton material and secure with a twisty-tie.

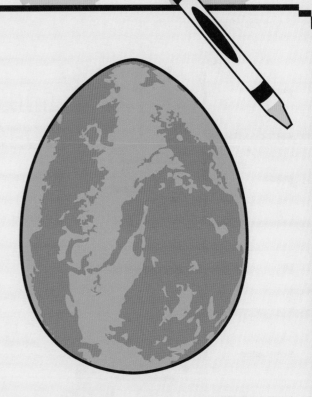

4. Bring a pan of water to the boil and add 50ml of white vinegar. Submerge the egg and boil for 20 minutes.

5. Remove from the pan and allow to cool before unwrapping your masterpiece.

FOOD COLOURING.

1. Place an egg in a water glass.

2. Fill the glass with water that goes about one quarter of the way up the egg. Add lots of drops of food colouring. Leave the egg for 15 minutes.

3. Add a little bit more water so the level is half way up the egg. Wait another 15 minutes.

4. Add more water so it covers three quarters of the egg. Wait 15 minutes, then completely submerge the egg with water. Wait a final 15 minutes before pouring the water away.

5. Rest the egg in the empty glass until it is dry. Your egg will have an amber colour effect.

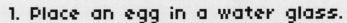

BOARD GAME

This game is like Snakes and Ladders. You will need a die and some game counters.

When you land on a pipe, slide down. When you land on the finger, tap up. Every time you land on a medal, flap forward an extra space.

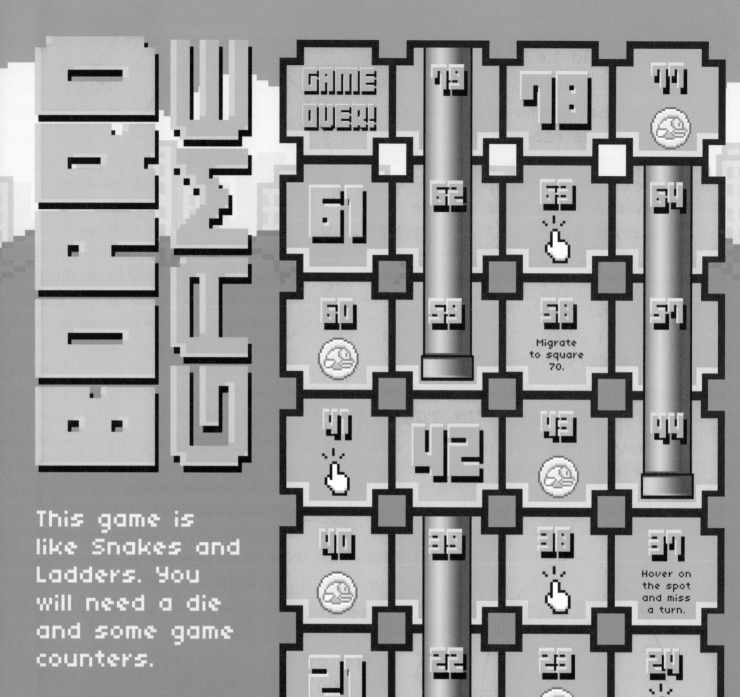

GAME OVER!

79

78

77

61

62

63

64

60

59

58
Migrate to square 70.

57

41

42

43

44

40

39

38

37
Hover on the spot and miss a turn.

21

22

23

24

20

19

18
Bounce back 2 spaces.

17

GET READY!!

2

3

4

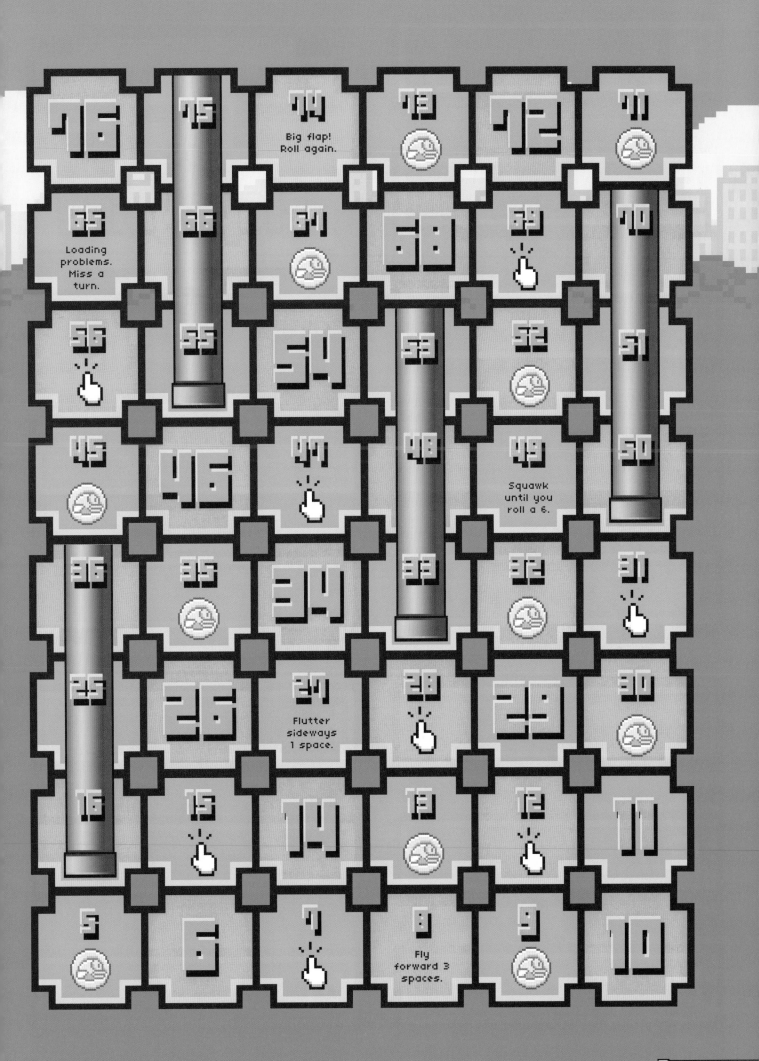

A is for app.

B is for bird.

C is for chirp.

D is for dangling pipes.

I is for imaginary world.

E is for eyes open.

J is for jetsetter.

F is for flappy.

K is for kids that love to play.

G is for get ready!

L is for little bird.

H is for hungry for medals.

M is for medal.

S is for score.

T is for tap.

U is for up.

N is for new start.

V is for very hard.

O is for over.

W is for wings.

P is for pixels.

X is for eXcellent aviator.

Q is for quick thinking.

Y is for year of flapping.

R is for repeat.

Z is for zero points.

ANSWERS

007 Birding About

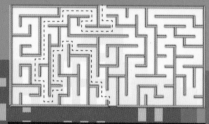

008 Tricky Turns

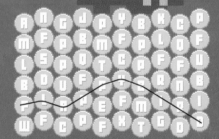

010 Chirpy Crossing

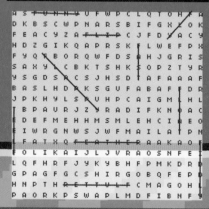

011 Feather Find

012 Silly Spotting

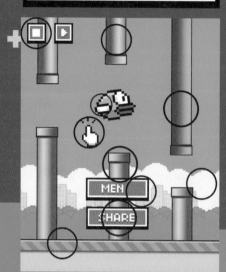

014 Pixelated Plumes

1. Parrot
2. Owl
3. Robin
4. Eagle
5. Crow
6. Flamingo

016 Counting Chaos

There are more medals than there are birds.

022 Odd Bird Out

1. Woodpecker
2. Parrot
3. Harris Hawk
4. Blue Tit

024 Odd Flappy Out

026 Flight Paths

The Answer is B

027 Migrating Muddle

The Answer is D

028 Rattled Letters

MEDAL   CLOUD

TAP   PIXEL

PIPE   SCORE

BIRD

029 Bird Song

CALL   CHIRP

HOOT   TRILL

TWEET   WARBLE

SING

029 Where in the world...

1. New York
2. London
3. Giza
4. Paris
5. Nepal
6. Pisa
7. Rio
8. Sydney

041 Sudoku Squak

054 Flappy Patterns

055 Game Glitch

The Answer is MEDAL.

058 Wild Bird Chase

060 Finders Keepers

074 Baby Birds

A. Swan   E. Blue Jay

B. Owl   F. Emu

C. Kestrel   G. Duck

D. Toucan   H. Peacock

076 Flappy Feet

Purple: 10 Medals

Orange: 6 Medals

Red: 8 Medals

083 Medal Tally

Gold: 10   Bronze: 11

Silver: 13   Fake: 7

086 Shattered Screens

A: 5   G: 8

B: 1   H: 14

C: 2   I: 11

D: 6   J: 9

E: 3   K: 10

F: 12

088 True or False

1. T   9. T

2. F   10. F

3. T   11. T

4. T   12. F

5. F   13. T

6. T   14. T

7. F   15. T

8. T

096 Flappy School

1. 12 Pipes

2. 19 Medals

3. 9 Games

4. 14 Taps

5. 40 Flaps

6. 16 Birds

096 Flappy School

1. Edinburgh Castle

2. White Cliffs of Dover

3. Blackpool Tower

4. Roman Baths

5. London Eye

6. Stonehenge

7. Snowdonia Mountains

8. Angel of the North